Heath Social Studies

Neighborhoods and Communities

Program Authors

Gloria P. Hagans Social Studies Coordinator, K–12, Norfolk Public Schools, Norfolk, Virginia.

Barbara Radner Reque Director, DePaul University Center for Economic Education, Chicago, Illinois.

Richard Hall Wilson Social Studies Coordinator, Montgomery County Public Schools, Rockville, Maryland; Instructor, American History, University of Maryland and Montgomery College.

Reading Consultants

Ted Schuder Coordinator, K–8 Reading/Language Arts Program, Montgomery County Public Schools, Rockville, Maryland.

Nan Jackson Reading/Language Arts Specialist, Montgomery County Public Schools, Rockville, Maryland.

Executive Editor Phyllis Goldstein
Freelance Assistance Susan T. Marx
Editorial Services Marianna Frew Palmer
Series Designer Robert H. Botsford

Reviewers

Virginia M. Bryant Social Studies Coordinator, Pascagoula (Mississippi) Municipal Separate School District.

Barbara H. Clinebell Teacher, Gratigny Elementary School, Miami, Florida.

Leah Engelhardt Professor, Curriculum and Instruction, Mississippi State University.

Nancy N. Galante Curriculum Specialist, Broward County (Florida) Public Schools.

Margo Martin Teacher, Lawrenceville Elementary School, Lawrenceville, Georgia.

James H. Rogers Former Social Studies Supervisor, Broward County (Florida) Public Schools.

Audrey B. Singleton Teacher, Herty Elementary School, Savannah, Georgia.

Heath Social Studies

Neighborhoods and Communities

Barbara Radner Reque

D.C. Heath and Company
Lexington, Massachusetts   Toronto

Contents

Unit One
Our Round Earth

We live on **Earth.** It is very big. The only way you can see all of Earth is to take a trip into space. Then you can see all of Earth.

Looking Down on Earth

From space you can see Earth. What shape is it?

What parts of Earth can you see? You
can see clouds in the air. Look again.
Can you see the water? What else can
you see?

To Help You Remember

1. What shape is Earth?
2. What parts of Earth can you see from
   space?

Looking at the Land

From space Earth looks like a big, blue ball. As you move closer to Earth, it looks different.

You can see the land better. You can see **mountains** on the land. A mountain is very high land. What do mountains look like?

You can see **hills.** How is a hill different from a mountain?

A hill is not as high as a mountain.

Some parts of Earth are flat. A **plain** is flat land. How is a plain different from mountains?

To Help You Remember

1. What kind of land is very high?
2. What kind of land is flat?
3. What is the land like where you live?

Looking at Lakes and Oceans

From space you saw water. That water is in **oceans.** Oceans cover much of Earth.

An ocean is a very large body of salt water. What lives in an ocean?

From space you cannot see **lakes.** A lake is smaller than an ocean. It is different in another way too. A lake is a body of water with land all around it.

To Help You Remember

1. Which is bigger, a lake or an ocean?
2. Which has land all around it, a lake or an ocean?

Looking at Rivers

A **river** is a stream of water. A river moves from high land to the ocean.

This river starts high in a mountain. It runs down the mountain side.

Then the river flows across the plain.
It moves more slowly now.

At last the river runs into the ocean.

mountain

hill

lake

river

plain

To Help You Remember

This picture shows where the river goes.
1. Where does the river start?
2. Where does the river go next?
3. Where does the river end?

ocean

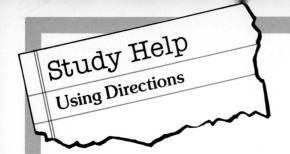
A **globe** is a model of our round Earth. It shows land and water. It can also help you find directions on Earth.

Use the picture of a globe, or use a real one. Find the North Pole. Now put your finger anywhere else on the globe. Move your finger toward the North Pole. Your finger is going north.

North is a direction. It means toward the North Pole. When you are going north, you are going toward the North Pole.

South is a direction too. It means toward the South Pole. Point to a place on the globe. Move south. Move toward the South Pole.

North

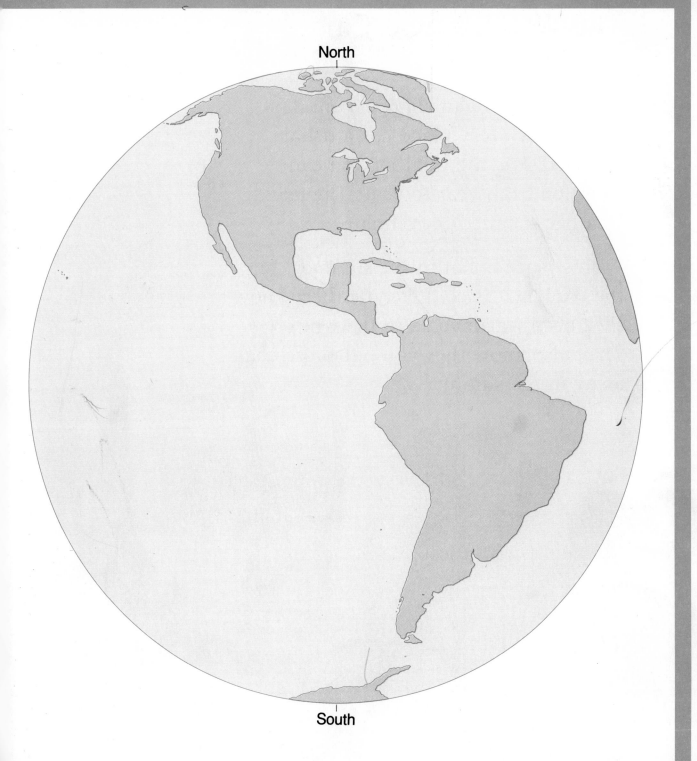

South

The Weather You Can Count On

The weather can change from day to day. Yet every place has a usual weather. It is the weather you can count on from year to year. The usual weather is called the **climate.**

This place is hot in the summer. In the winter, it is cold. People there know they need warm coats in the winter. They also know they can put those coats away in the summer.

This picture shows a place near the
South Pole. Snow stays on the ground
all year. This place has a cold climate.
What lives there?

This place is sunny and hot all year. It gets little rain. It has a hot, dry climate. What lives there?

Here it is warm all year. Plenty of rain falls. This place has a warm, wet climate.

To Help You Remember

1. What is climate?
2. What is the climate like where you live?

Using Earth

Everyone uses Earth. A part of Earth people use is called a **resource.**

Trees are a resource. Wood and paper come from trees. What do you use that comes from trees?

Water is a resource. How do you use
water?

Some resources come from deep in the ground. Coal is that kind of resource. Some people use coal to keep their homes warm.

The sun keeps Earth warm. People use the heat of the sun as a resource. The sun keeps this home warm.

To Help You Remember

1. What is a resource?
2. Name a resource. Tell how you use the resource.

Taking Care of Earth

People need resources to live. It is important to take care of them.

People cut down trees. Then they plant new trees. This way there will always be enough for others to use.

Everyone needs water. Keeping water clean is important.

These people are cleaning up water. When they are done, fish can live in the water. The water will be good for swimming. The water will be good to drink.

To Help You Remember

1. Why do people plant new trees?
2. Why do people keep water clean?
3. How can you take care of resources?

Unit Review

Words to Know

1. Match the words to the letters on the
   picture. Write each word on your paper.

   ocean   mountain   plain
   lake   river   hill

   A. _____
   B. _____
   C. _____
   D. _____
   E. _____
   F. _____

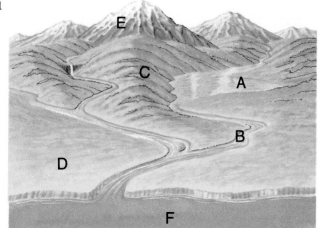

2. Find two resources in the picture.
   Tell how each resource is used.
   What is climate?

3. What is a globe?
   What letter shows the North Pole?
   What letter shows the South Pole?

Reviewing Main Ideas

Finish each sentence.
Write the sentences on your paper.

1. We live on ___ .   climate
2. Water is a ___ .   Earth
3. The usual weather is the ___ .   resource

Keeping Skills Sharp

You are going toward the North Pole.
In which direction are you going?

You are going toward the South Pole.
In which direction are you going?

Challenge!

Tell about the place where you live.
What is the land like? What resources
are around you? What kind of water is
near you? What is your climate like?

Unit Two
Building a Community

A **community** is a place where people live and work and play. People use resources to build a community. This is the story of a family. The people in the family helped to build a community long ago.

35

Moving to Pigeon Creek

At first, the Lincoln family lived in Kentucky. There was Abe, who was seven, and Sarah, who was nine. Nancy was their mother. Thomas was their father.

The Lincolns wanted more land. So they decided to move to Pigeon Creek. Pigeon Creek was a village in Indiana.

The family brought some things they
needed. They had some tools and a pot
for cooking. They had clothes and a
horse too.

The trip was long and hard. First, the Lincolns walked beside their horse. Then they went across a river on a boat. Then they walked some more. At last, they came to Pigeon Creek.

To Help You Remember

1. Why did the Lincoln family go to Pigeon Creek?
2. What did they bring to Pigeon Creek?

Working Together

It was winter when the Lincoln family came to Pigeon Creek. It was cold. The family needed many things.

The Lincolns needed a home. The family used the resources on their land. Trees grew on the land. The Lincolns made their house out of logs from the trees.

The family needed a fire for cooking.
Abe and Sarah got wood for the fire.

The family needed water. The
children carried water from the river.
They had to carry it a long way.

In the spring, the Lincolns worked hard. First, they cut down trees. Then they planted corn. They picked it in the fall.

After the corn was picked, neighbors came to the family's home. They had a corn husking bee. Two teams raced to see which could peel the corn faster.

To Help You Remember

1. What did the Lincoln family need to live?
2. How did the family get the things it needed?

41

The Lincolns had their corn ground at a mill. Abe took the corn there.

A **map** is a drawing of a place. This map shows where the mill was. The map also shows how Abe got there.

A map **key** helps you read the map. The key tells you what map **symbols** mean. A symbol is a line, dot, or picture that stands for a real thing.

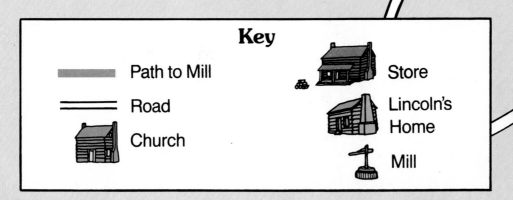

Key

Path to Mill

Road

Church

Store

Lincoln's Home

Mill

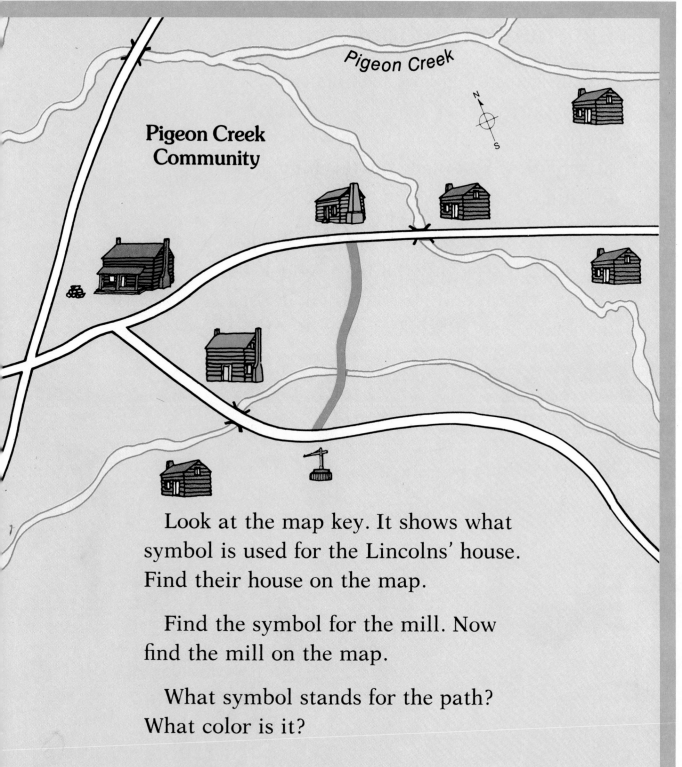

Pigeon Creek

Pigeon Creek Community

Look at the map key. It shows what symbol is used for the Lincolns' house. Find their house on the map.

Find the symbol for the mill. Now find the mill on the map.

What symbol stands for the path? What color is it?

Learning at School

Children in Pigeon Creek learned many things. They learned from their mothers and fathers. They also learned at **school.** It is a place for teaching and learning.

When Abe was nine, a teacher started a school. It was called a blab school. In a blab school, children say their lessons out loud. They all talk at once.

Children wrote their lessons. They used feathers as pens. They used ink made from berries.

To Help You Remember

1. What was a blab school like?
2. How did the children write their lessons?

At the Store

One year a man opened a **store** near
Pigeon Creek. A store is a place that
sells things. The store sold such things
as needles, salt, and cooking pots. These
are things people did not make at home.

46

Some people paid for these things with money. But most people would **trade** or exchange one thing for another. A farmer might trade corn for salt. Another farmer might trade bacon for a needle.

47

Abe worked in the store. He helped people trade for things they needed. Abe learned about other cities and towns at the store. He talked to people who had been to other places. He also read newspapers. The newspapers came from places far away.

When Abe grew older, he would live in one of those faraway places. He would be president of the United States. He would live in Washington, D.C.

To Help You Remember

1. What did people do at the store?
2. How did people buy things at the store?

Unit Review

Words to Know

A. Tell why each is important in a community.

store   trade   school

B. Tell how a key and a symbol help us to read a map.

Reviewing Main Ideas

Draw three pictures. Show how people lived in Pigeon Creek.

1. Show how people traded one thing for another.

2. Show how children learned to read and write.

3. Show how neighbors helped each other.

Keeping Skills Sharp

Finish the key.

Draw the key on your paper.

Key	
Store	School
Path	House
Mill	Road

Challenge!

Pretend you came here to live. There is no store nearby.

1. What would you need?
2. What resources would you use?
3. How would you build your house?
4. What would you eat?

Unit Three
Living in a Farm Community

This is part of a **farm** community today. Animals are raised on a farm. Crops are grown there too. How is the farm community like Pigeon Creek long ago? How is it different?

52

Living on a Farm

A family uses the resources of the land to grow food. Near the house, there is a garden. The family grows some of its food in the garden.

The family raises some pigs. The family also keeps chickens. The children collect the eggs. Their mother sells them in **town.** A town is a small community where people live and work.

The family grows corn on most of its land. How can one family grow so much corn? Machines help the family do the work.

In the spring, the farmer uses a machine for plowing. The machine digs up the soil. It gets the soil ready for planting.

Another machine helps to plant seeds.

In the fall, the farmer picks the corn. A machine helps with that job too.

A farmer is a **producer.** A producer makes or grows something. Many farmers produce corn.

Farmers sell some of their corn crop. They sell it to people in town.

Farmers sell most of their crop to people in other communities. The farmers get money for the corn.

To Help You Remember

1. What work does a farm family do?
2. What happens to the corn the farmer grows?

Shopping

Farm families often live far from each other. They may live far from the town too. They drive in to town for things they need. Here farmers buy things they do not produce. They use the money they got for the corn.

Along the main street of the town there are many stores. Some stores sell food. Other stores sell clothes. There is a place to buy farm machines. There is also a place where those machines are fixed.

Many people work in these places. These workers help people get the things they need. A person who does work that helps others is called a **service worker.**

To Help You Remember

1. What kinds of stores do the farmers find in town?
2. Name some ways service workers help people.

Working for the Community

Some service workers help their community. The police are service workers. Firefighters and teachers are also service workers. So are people who work on roads. The town pays these workers.

People pay money to their town. They pay **taxes.** A tax is money that the town uses.

Tax money helps to pay community helpers. Taxes also help to pay for schools.

To Help You Remember

1. How is tax money used?
2. Name some service workers and tell what they do.

Tax money pays for schools.
It pays for books. It also pays for buses.

In some places, many towns help pay for one school. Look at the map. It shows the towns that send their children to one school. Name the towns.

Elmville

The arrows on the map tell you directions. The arrows point to north and south. The arrows tell you that Hilltown is north of the school. Which town is south of the school?

The arrows also point to east and west. They are also directions. **East** is the direction to your right when you face north. The direction to your left when you face north is **west.** Bus A drives east after school. To which two towns does it go? Bus B goes west. Name the town it goes to.

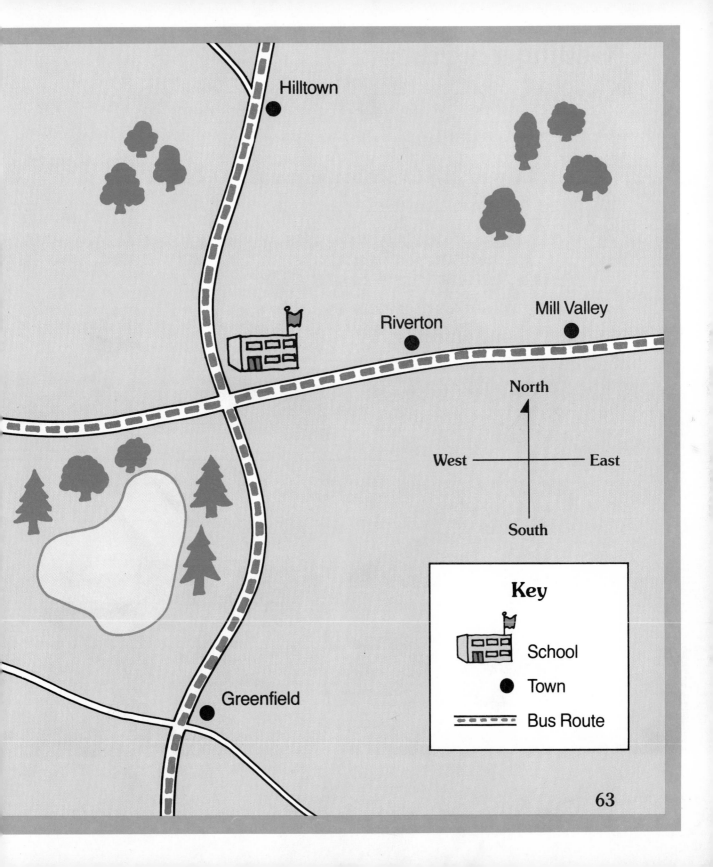

Hilltown

Riverton

Mill Valley

North

West — East

South

Greenfield

Key

School

● Town

===== Bus Route

63

Getting Together

A farm town has many places where farmers get together.

Some farmers go to school at night. They go to learn about new ways to grow crops.

Children belong to a 4-H club. The children are showing what they have learned about animals.

Every year there is a fair. Farm families show the food and animals they have raised. Everyone enjoys the games and rides.

To Help You Remember

1. Where do people in a farm family get together?
2. What do they learn?

Unit Review

Words to Know

A. Finish each sentence.
Write the sentences on your paper.

1. A farmer is a ___.
   producer   service worker
2. The direction to your left when you
   face north is ___.
   east   west
3. A small community where people live
   and work is a ___.
   town   farm

B. What is a tax?
How do taxes help the community?

Reviewing Main Ideas

Draw a picture of a service worker and
a producer in a farm community. Tell
what each person does.

Keeping Skills Sharp

Follow the directions. Help the children find the surprise on the farm.

Challenge!

Draw a map of your own. Hide a surprise. Give directions to help find your surprise.

Start at the house.

Go east to the barn.

Now go south. What do you find?

Turn to the west. Go to the horse.

Now go north. Find the surprise!

A **city** is a community. It is a big, busy place. Many people live and work in a big city.

69

A Big City

City families live close together. Some families live in apartments. Their homes are in a tall building. Some of their neighbors live in other apartments in the same building. Other neighbors live in houses nearby.

Cities change. People fix up old buildings. People also build new ones.

The people in the picture are making
a new building. It will be a place for
people to live and work and shop. There
will be apartments and stores in it.

To Help You Remember

1. What are homes like in a city?
2. How do cities change?

Working in a City

SHIPPING ROOM

FREIGHT ONLY

Quality DRESS CO.

Quality DRESS CO.

PLEASE USE OTHER DOOR

Quality DRESS CO.

10 DOZ ZIPPS   HANDI-BUTTON

There are many jobs in a city. Some people work in a **factory.** These people are producers. Factory workers use machines to make things. In some factories, people make clothes. In other factories, people make computers.

People also work in offices. Many of them do work that helps others. They are service workers.

Some people type letters. Some clean teeth. Others make plans for new homes and factories. What else do office workers do?

To Help You Remember

1. What jobs are producers doing?
2. What jobs are service workers doing?

Getting to Work

City people **travel** to work in many ways. Travel means to go from place to place. They walk. They ride in cars. They ride a bus. They may also take the train.

Some people travel under the ground. They take the subway.

Bus drivers are service workers. The people who work on the trains and subways are also service workers. They all help people get from place to place in the city.

To Help You Remember

1. How do people travel in a city?
2. What service workers help people travel in a city?

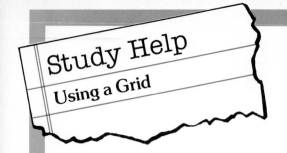

This map is a street map. It shows part of a city.

The streets divide the city into blocks. You can see the blocks on the map. You can see corners where two streets cross. Find the place where First Street crosses A Street. What building is there?

Start at Lincoln School. Go to the store. It is two blocks from the school to the store.

The second grade is going to the fire house. How many blocks is it from the school to the fire house? Will the children go north or south?

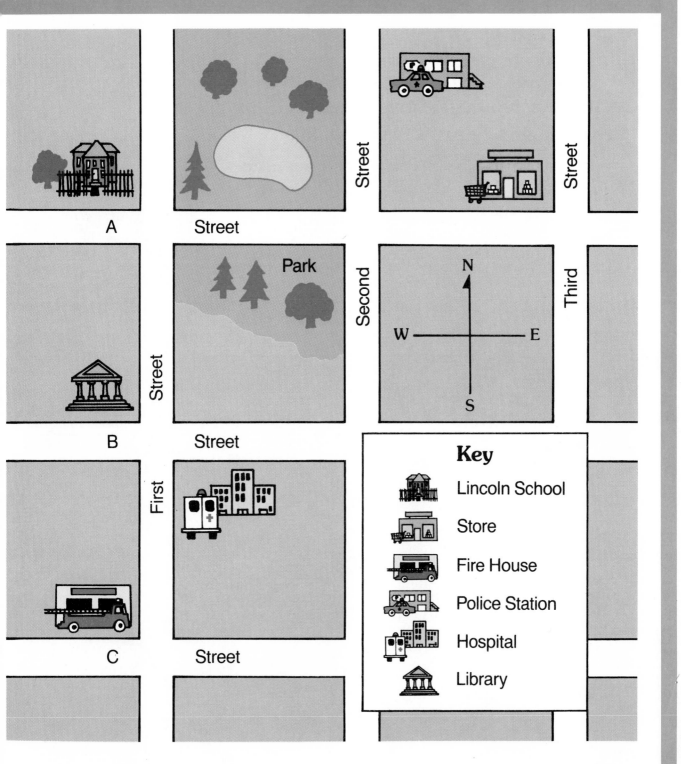

A

Street

Street

Park

Second

Third

Street

N

W —— E

S

B

Street

First

C

Street

Street

Key

Lincoln School

Store

Fire House

Police Station

Hospital

Library

Shopping

Every day many people shop in the city. A person who buys things is a **consumer.** Factory workers, office workers, and bus drivers are consumers. They buy things they need.

Consumers buy and use **goods.** Goods are things people make or grow. Food and clothes are goods.

Consumers buy and use services too. They have their hair cut. They eat a meal.

DIRECTORY

1ST FLOOR
- SANDWICH SHOP
- SPORTING GOODS
- TOYS · GAMES

2ND FLOOR
- HAIR SALON
- LADIES WEAR
- SHOES

3RD FLOOR
- LAMPS · FURNITU

SANDWICH SHOP

TOYS · GAM

JUMP ROPES

· PLEASE · WATCH YOUR STEP!

78

Sometimes consumers buy things in a big store. Shoppers find goods there. They find services too. They buy clothes and toys. They get a haircut. They use a list to find where things are.

To Help You Remember

1. What are people who buy and use goods and services called?
2. What goods and services can you find in the store on this page?

79

Unit Review

Words to Know
Look at these pictures.

1. Find the factory workers. They are producers. What goods are they making?
2. Find the consumer. What does a consumer do?
3. Find ways to travel. What type of community is it?

Reviewing Main Ideas
Make a picture of a city. Put these buildings in your picture.

factory   office building   store

Put people in the picture too.

service worker   consumer   producer

Keeping Skills Sharp

1. A bus driver is going to work at the bus station. How many blocks will she travel to get there?
2. A builder is going to work at a new building. How many blocks will he travel?

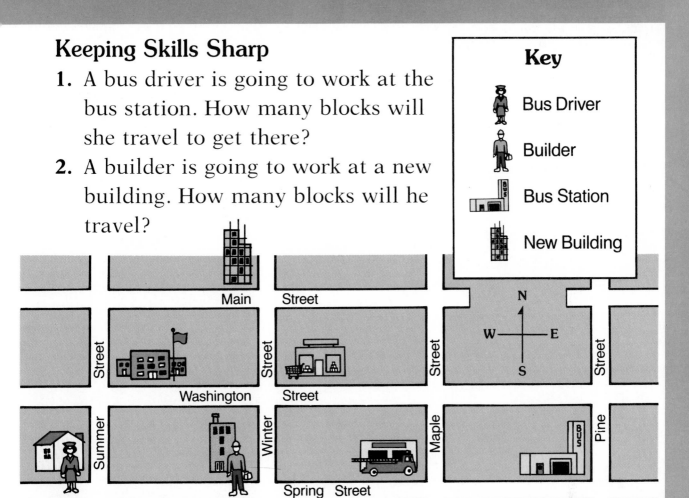

Challenge!

Tell the answer to this riddle.

I have a house and a barn.
My neighbors live far from me.
I grow vegetables.
Where do I live?

Now write a riddle about the city.

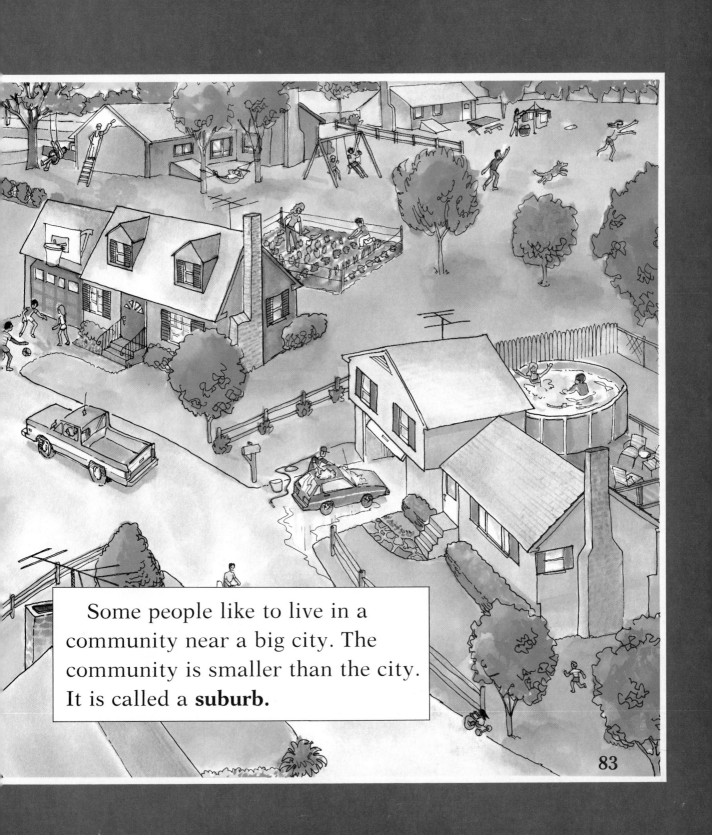

Some people like to live in a community near a big city. The community is smaller than the city. It is called a **suburb.**

Near the City

The city is important to people in a
suburb. Some people go to work in the
city every day. They go to the city by
train. They may go by bus or car. These
people are **commuters.** A commuter is a
person who travels to work.

People in a suburb get some news from a city. Their newspaper comes from the city. They also watch TV programs that come from the city.

People in a suburb use the city airport. Sometimes Grandmother comes to visit. Then her family drives to the city in a car. The family meets her at the airport.

Sometimes, a family takes a bus to the city. The family may see a baseball game. It may go to the circus.

To Help You Remember

1. What do you call people who live in a suburb and work in a city?
2. How is the city important to people in a suburb?

The children in this class live in the suburbs. Some family members work close to home. They work in the suburbs.

Other family members have jobs in the city. They travel to their jobs. They are commuters.

A graph can help us compare things.
It shows how family members travel
to their jobs in the city.

Look at the graph.
Then answer the questions.

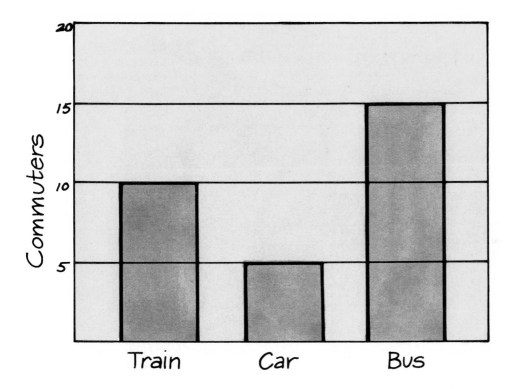

1. How many family members travel by train?
2. How do five family members travel?
3. How do most family members travel
   to the city?

Choosing a Home

A family is moving. It is leaving a small town. The mother has a new job in a big city.

The family must choose where to live. The mother wants to live near her job. She also wants a place for a garden. The children want a big yard to play in.

First, the family looks at homes in the city. Then the family looks at homes in the suburbs.

The family decides to buy a house in a
suburb. The house has a big yard. There
is a train to the city. The mother can
ride to work on it.

To Help You Remember

1. Why did the family move?
2. Why did the family choose to live in
   a suburb?

Pipes and Wires

In the new home, the family needs many things. The family needs water. It comes through pipes to the house. The family pays the community to get the water it uses.

The family needs a telephone. A telephone company puts in wires for a new phone. The telephone company has many wires. Those wires link the family to many other places.

To Help You Remember

1. How does the family get water?
2. What else comes to the house through pipes and wires?

Key

Water	
Electricity	
Telephone	
Sewage	

Citizens

A person who lives in a community is a **citizen** of that community. Good citizens help their community. They keep it clean. They also obey its rules.

A law is a rule of a community. The pictures show some of the rules in a community.

Grown-up citizens **vote.** To vote is to
make a choice. Citizens choose people to
make laws. They choose other leaders
too. These leaders see that the laws are
obeyed.

To Help You Remember
1. What do good citizens do?
2. How do citizens choose leaders?

Choices

Some communities have planning meetings. At these meetings citizens hear plans for their town. Then the citizens decide what to do.

Some citizens have to make a choice. They live in a suburb with many homes. A company wants to build an office building there. It will bring many jobs to the suburbs. Many people want the new building.

Other people do not want the office building. They say that it will take up too much land. It will bring too many cars and trucks to the suburb.

The citizens speak at the meeting. They listen too. They share their ideas. Then they choose the idea they like the best.

The graph shows how people voted. Seven people voted "yes." They want the office building. Only five people voted "no." They do not want the office building. Will the company be able to build the office building?

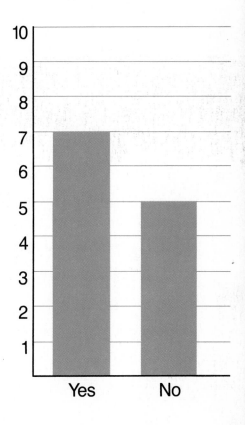

To Help You Remember

1. Tell why some people want the office building.
2. Tell why other people do not want it.

Unit Review

Words to Know

Write these words on a piece of paper.

1. vote   **3.** citizen   **5.** suburb
2. law   **4.** commuter

Now turn to **Words to Know** at the back of this book. It starts on page 162. It tells you what words mean. Find the five words. Read the meaning of each of these words. Then write each word in a sentence.

Reviewing Main Ideas

Draw three pictures. Show people in a suburb.

1. Show commuters going to work.
2. Show citizens voting at a planning meeting.
3. Show a family moving into a house. Then write a sentence telling about each picture.

Keeping Skills Sharp

The class voted on where to go on their trip. The graph shows how they voted. How many children want to go to the city? How many children want to visit a farm? Where will the class go?

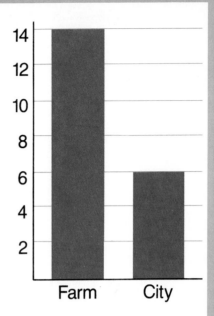

Challenge!

These signs show some community rules. Make a sign that shows one of the rules in your community.

Unit Six
Living in Our Country

These people live in a community. Their community is in a **country.** That country is the United States. A country is a land with its own laws and flag.

101

Our Country

The United States is a very big country. It has 50 parts. Each part is called a **state.**

Many people live in the United States. Some live on farms. Some live in big cities. Others live in suburbs. They are all citizens of their city or town. They are also citizens of their country. They are Americans.

When citizens see the **flag,** they think about their country. A flag is a piece of cloth that stands for a country. The flag of the United States has 50 stars. There is one star for each state.

Citizens say a pledge to the flag. They say that they are proud to be citizens of the United States.

To Help You Remember

1. What is the United States?
2. Why does the United States flag have 50 stars?

The map shows the United States. Find your state on the map. What is north of it? What is south of it? What is west of it? What is east of it?

Some states are very small. Find three small states on the map.

Some states are beside an ocean. Find four states by the Pacific Ocean. Now find four states by the Atlantic Ocean.

Choose a state you would like to visit. Tell the states you would cross to get to that state. In which direction would you go, north, south, east, or west?

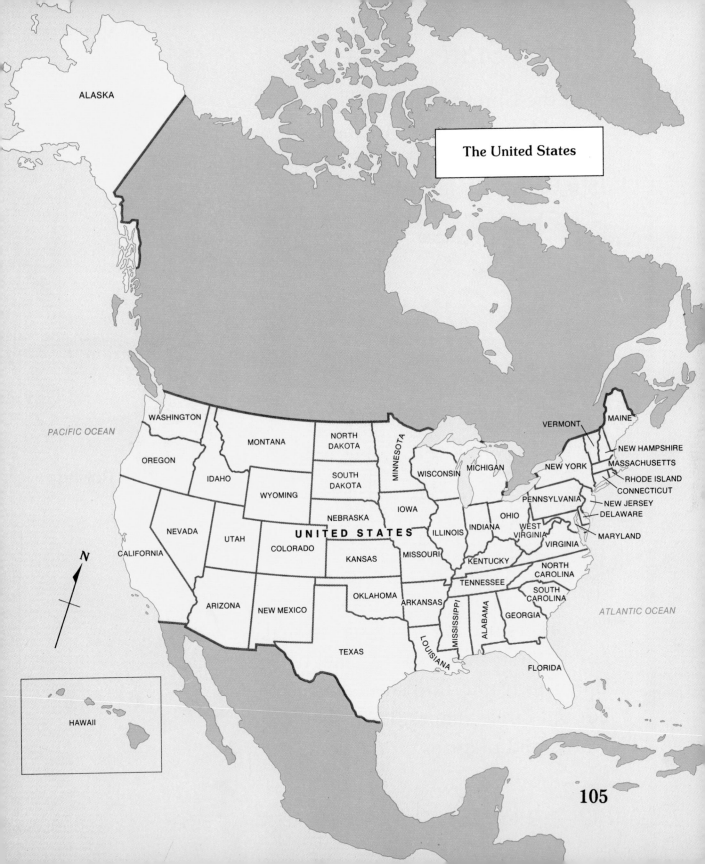

The United States

ALASKA

PACIFIC OCEAN

WASHINGTON

OREGON

IDAHO

MONTANA

NORTH DAKOTA

SOUTH DAKOTA

WYOMING

MINNESOTA

WISCONSIN

MICHIGAN

VERMONT

MAINE

NEW HAMPSHIRE

MASSACHUSETTS

RHODE ISLAND

CONNECTICUT

NEW YORK

PENNSYLVANIA

NEW JERSEY

DELAWARE

MARYLAND

N

NEVADA

UTAH

COLORADO

NEBRASKA

IOWA

UNITED STATES

ILLINOIS

INDIANA

OHIO

WEST VIRGINIA

VIRGINIA

CALIFORNIA

KANSAS

MISSOURI

KENTUCKY

NORTH CAROLINA

ARIZONA

NEW MEXICO

OKLAHOMA

ARKANSAS

TENNESSEE

SOUTH CAROLINA

GEORGIA

ATLANTIC OCEAN

MISSISSIPPI

ALABAMA

TEXAS

LOUISIANA

FLORIDA

HAWAII

105

United States Money

In the United States, people use the same kind of money. All the coins are made in a special place. They are made in a United States mint.

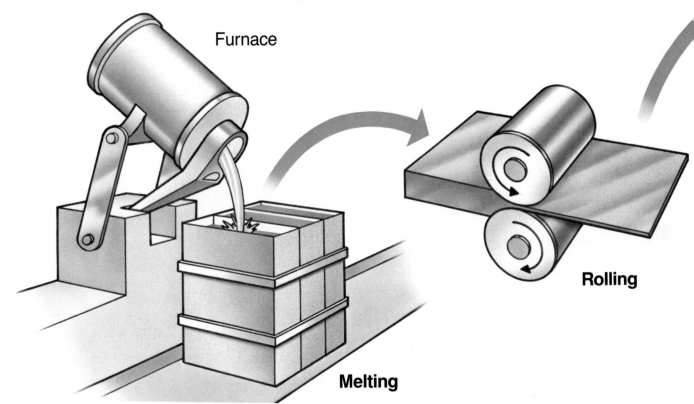

Furnace

Melting

Rolling

Workers use big machines to make coins. First, they melt the metal. Then they roll it into thin sheets. Next, they cut out circle shapes. Last, they stamp words and pictures on the coins.

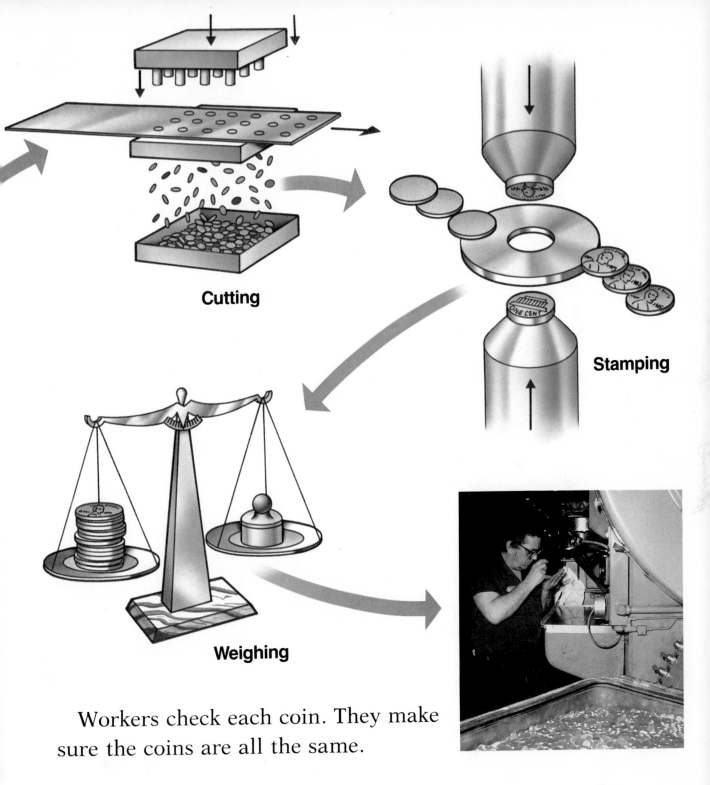

Cutting

Stamping

Weighing

Workers check each coin. They make sure the coins are all the same.

Look at these coins. How do you know they are United States money?

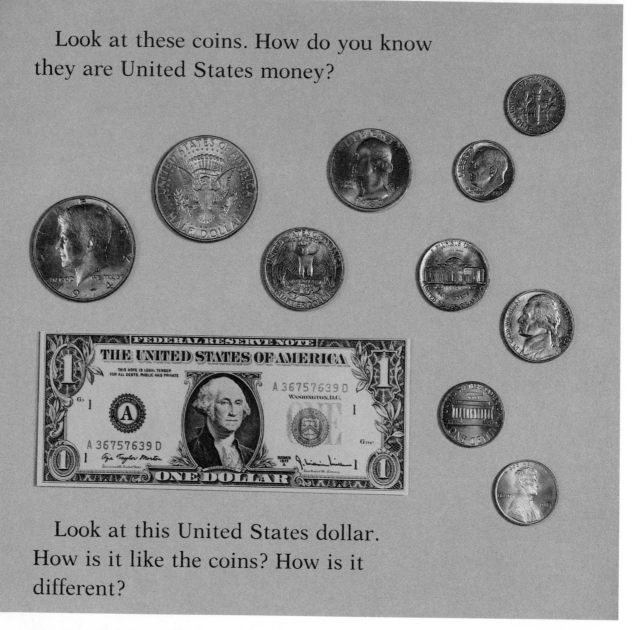

Look at this United States dollar. How is it like the coins? How is it different?

To Help You Remember

1. Where are United States coins made?
2. Name two kinds of coins.

United States Mail

All over the United States, people use the mail. They send letters to people. They send packages too. People use stamps to pay for sending a letter or package.

These pictures show stamps. They are all used in the United States. Each of these stamps has a price on it. Each one also has words and pictures.

Stamps tell about our country. They show important people. They show plants and animals. What else do they show?

109

People can buy stamps at the post office. They pay money for the stamps.

The post office uses that money. It pays the people who carry the mail.

To Help You Remember

1. Why do people use stamps?
2. Look at the pictures on the page. What jobs are post office workers doing?

United States Laws

Our country has rules, or laws. There is a law about voting. That law says that any citizen who is 18 years old or older can vote.

Citizens vote for the **president.** The president is the person who leads the United States government. They also vote for other leaders.

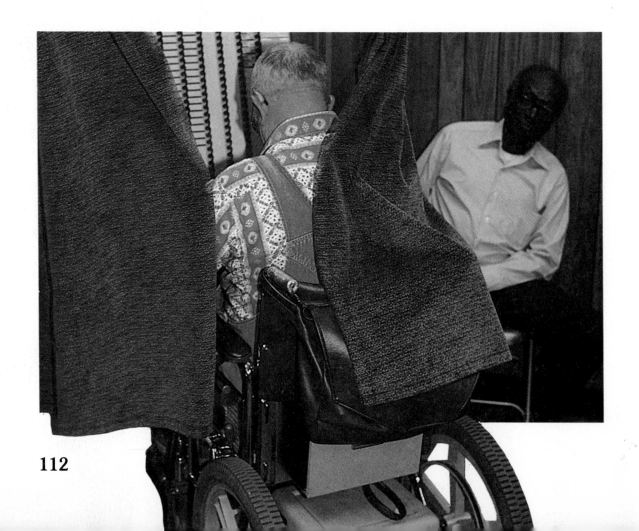

Our country has other laws too. It has laws about the flag. These laws are called the flag code.

The flag code says the flag should fly during the day, but it should be taken down at night. The flag code says the flag should fly at post offices.

To Help You Remember

1. How old must you be to vote?
2. What is the flag code?

United States Holidays

Everyone in the United States shares holidays. The Fourth of July is a holiday. That day is the birthday of the United States.

Presidents' Day is also a holiday. On that day people remember two American leaders. Americans remember George Washington. He was the first president of the United States.

Americans also remember Abraham Lincoln. He was president long after Washington. While he was president, the country faced a big problem. Two parts of the United States were at war with each other. Lincoln worked to bring the country together again.

To Help You Remember

1. Why is the Fourth of July a holiday?
2. Why is Presidents' Day a holiday?

Unit Review

Words to Know

Choose the right word for the end of each sentence.

1. The United States is a ___.
2. We say a pledge to the ___.
3. People in the United States vote for the ___.
4. Each part of the United States is a ___.

    a. country
    b. president
    c. state
    d. flag

Reviewing Main Ideas

Which sentence tells about the picture?

1. a. George Washington was the first president of the United States.
   b. Abraham Lincoln was president of the United States.

2. a. Citizens vote for the leaders of the country.
   b. Our country has laws about the flag.

3. a. Coins are made at a United States mint.

b. People buy stamps at the post office.

Keeping Skills Sharp

Look at the map.

Then answer the questions.

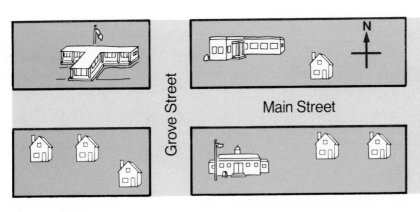

1. What is north of the post office?
2. What is west of the library?
3. In which direction do you go from the school to the library?

Challenge!

Find out more about our first president.

Give a report to the class.

Goods and ideas go from place to place. **Transportation** is a way of moving things from place to place. What do you see that helps goods to travel? What helps ideas travel?

119

Trading Resources

Resources are the things people use. Every community has some of the resources it needs. No community has all the resources it needs. So every community trades with other communities.

A city is near the ocean. People there catch many fish. They eat some of these fish. Then they still have more fish than they need.

People near the ocean sell their extra fish.
They use some of the money to buy beef.

There is not much land near the city for raising beef cattle. People buy their beef from another community. Ranchers there have much land. They raise big herds of cattle on **ranches.** A ranch is a large farm where animals are raised and crops are grown. They sell the beef to people in other places. They sell some of it to people in the ocean community.

To Help You Remember

1. Why do people in the ocean community sell their fish?
2. Why do they have to buy beef?

Trucks and Trains

How does beef get from a ranch to other places? Trucks and trains do the job. Day and night they cross the country. They bring every community things it needs.

Highways and railroad tracks join cities and towns. They go from one community to another.

Sometimes goods are carried on a truck and a train at the same time. Trucks ride piggyback on the train. Workers load a truck trailer full of goods on a railroad car. The trailer rides on the train.

Sometimes truck trailers travel another way. They ride on boats. Trucks, trains, and boats work together to carry goods.

To Help You Remember

1. How do goods get to places in all parts of the country?
2. How do goods get to your community?

Boats

Many kinds of boats carry goods. Boats use oceans and lakes and rivers as highways.

The Mississippi River is like a big highway. Coal and corn and wood ride up and down the river.

Barges carry goods on the Mississippi. Barges are flat boats. They have no engines. Towboats push them. A towboat can push many barges at one time.

To Help You Remember
1. What do boats use as highways?
2. What kind of goods do boats carry?

Pipelines

Oil is a resource. Every community needs it. People use it to run machines. People also use it to keep homes warm.

Trucks and trains and boats carry oil. Oil also travels another way. It goes through pipes.

Miles and miles of pipes carry oil across the country. These pipes are called a **pipeline.** Some of the pipes are under the ground. Some are above the ground. Others are under the water.

To Help You Remember

1. Name four ways oil travels.
2. Where are three places that pipelines can be found?

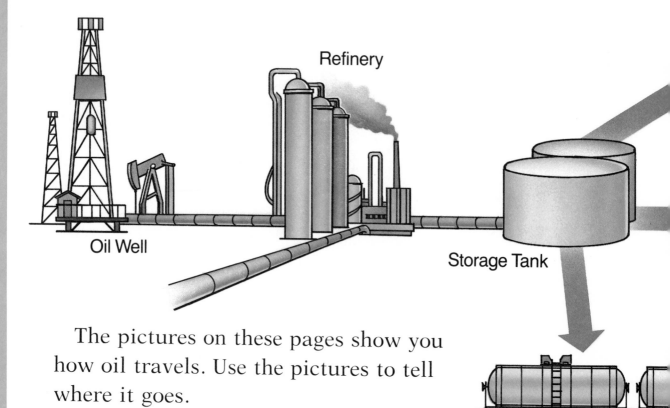

Refinery

Oil Well

Storage Tank

The pictures on these pages show you how oil travels. Use the pictures to tell where it goes.

Oil comes from wells. Workers dig wells in the ground. They pump the oil up above the ground. They pump it into pipes. The oil goes through the pipes to a special factory. There the oil is made into gasoline.

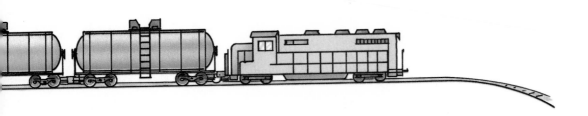

The gasoline leaves the factory.

Use the pictures. Tell where the gasoline goes from the factory. Where do the trucks take the gasoline?

Airplanes

Airplanes fly very fast. They can go hundreds of miles in an hour. Sometimes goods have to get to a place fast. Then they are sent by airplane.

Workers pack goods in boxes. Packing boxes are made to fit the inside of the airplane. No space is wasted.

Fresh flowers are put in boxes. These boxes are like big refrigerators. They keep the flowers cool and fresh.

Sometimes zoo animals fly in airplanes. The animals are put in boxes. The boxes keep them safe. People from a zoo stay with the animals. These people take care of the animals.

To Help You Remember

1. What kinds of goods are sent by plane?
2. How are goods packed for flying?

Getting the News

News travels too. There are many ways for people to find out what is happening.

An animal is born at the zoo. The zoo keeper wants people to know. She calls reporters on the telephone. The call goes through telephone wires.

Reporters come to the zoo. They ask questions about the baby. Then they write stories about it.

Some reporters work for newspapers. The newspapers print the story on paper. Trucks then carry the newspapers to many cities and towns. People buy the papers. They read the news about the baby at the zoo.

Other reporters read the story on radio and TV. Towers at the stations send signals through the air. People get the signals when they turn on their radios or TV's. They also learn the news.

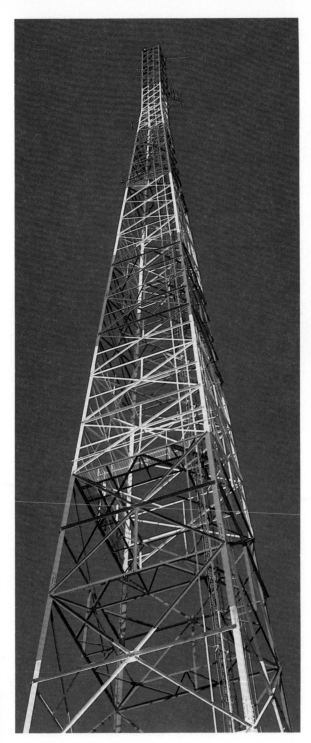

To Help You Remember

1. What do reporters do?
2. Name three ways people get the news.
3. How do you get the news?

Unit Review

Words to Know

1. Name three kinds of transportation.
2. Name a way oil travels.
3. Name a place with much land.

Reviewing Main Ideas

Find the right words for the end of each sentence. Write the sentences on your paper.

1. A ranch
2. A pipeline
3. A newspaper
4. An airplane

a. carries oil across the country.
b. brings goods fast to a place.
c. tells people what is happening.
d. is a large farm with animals or crops.

Keeping Skills Sharp

Make your own diagram.

1. Show flowers being grown.
2. Show flowers being packed in boxes.
3. Show boxes being loaded on an airplane.
4. Show boxes being delivered to store.

Challenge!

Read the newspaper story. Then answer the questions.

1. WHO is it about?
2. WHAT happened?
3. WHERE did it happen?
4. WHEN did it happen?

22 THE CHRONICLE   SEPTEMBER 5, 19

A New Baby

Something very exciting happened at the zoo on Monday. Elly the Elephant had a baby girl. The little elephant weighs 200 pounds. The mother and baby are doing well.

Elly the Elephant ha
t the z

Unit Eight
Around the World

There are many countries on Earth. Each country has its own land. Each country has its own flag. Together, countries can share the resources of Earth.

141

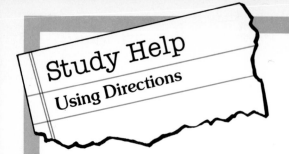

Study Help

Using Directions

This map shows land and water. A large body of land is called a **continent.** It has water all around it. North America is a continent. Find it on the map.

What continent is south of North America?

There are three big countries in North America. The country you live in is one of them. Find the country you live in.

Canada is also a country. Find Canada.

Now find another country. Find the country that is south of the United States.

CANADA

NORTH AMERICA

UNITED STATES

MEXICO

N
W E
S

SOUTH AMERICA

143

Trading Partners

Mexico is a country on the continent of North America. Mexico has a warm climate.

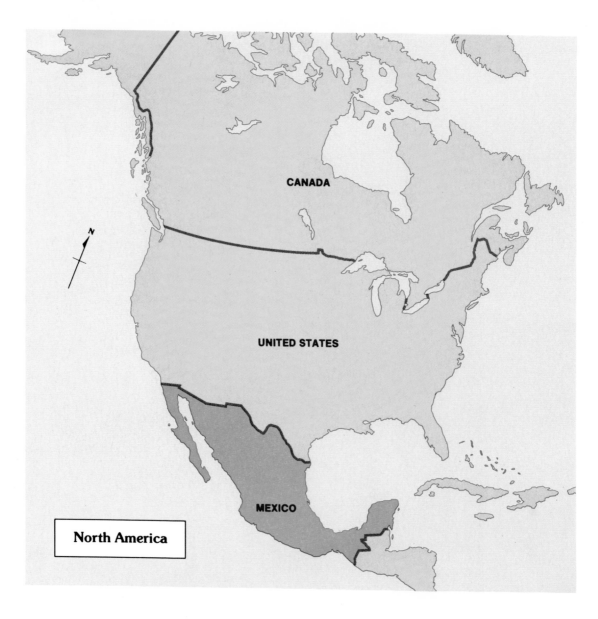

CANADA

UNITED STATES

MEXICO

North America

The United States is also on the continent of North America. Parts of the United States are very cold in winter.

People in cold places want to eat fresh tomatoes all year. Tomatoes grow in warm weather. Some of these tomatoes come from Mexico. In Mexico, it is warm enough to grow tomatoes all year long.

There is a big farm machine factory in the United States. Workers there make tractors and plows. Many of these farm machines are sold in Mexico.

Mexico and the United States are **trading partners.** The two countries buy and sell goods. They help each other.

To Help You Remember

1. Why do countries buy resources?
2. Why do countries sell resources?

Working Together

Canada is a country in North America. Canada and the United States work together.

The Saint Lawrence is a river. It runs between the United States and Canada. It starts in the Great Lakes. It goes to the Atlantic Ocean. Find the Saint Lawrence River on the map.

Years ago, big ships could travel on the ocean. They could also travel on the Great Lakes. They could not travel from the ocean to the Great Lakes, though.

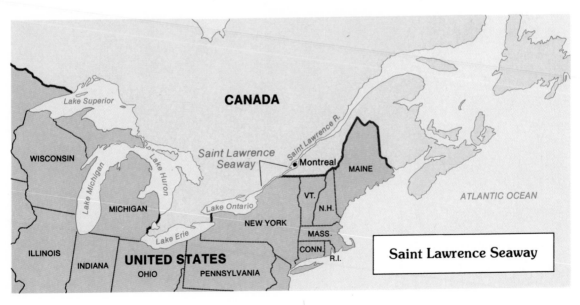

Saint Lawrence Seaway

The United States and Canada decided to work together. They planned a way for ocean ships to reach the Great Lakes. They built the Saint Lawrence Seaway. It was wide and deep enough for big ships.

Now big ships can go from the Great
Lakes to the ocean. Big ships can also
go from the ocean to the Great Lakes.
They carry goods to the United States.
They also carry goods to Canada.

To Help You Remember

1. Why did the United States and
   Canada want the Saint Lawrence
   Seaway?
2. How does the seaway help both
   countries?

Sharing with Other Countries

Children in many countries belong to the Girl Scouts or Boy Scouts. Their uniforms look different. They speak different languages. Yet when they get together, they all have fun.

Sometimes, Scouts from many places get together. They set up tents. They cook their own food.

Scouts talk about their own country. They learn about life in other countries too. They talk about their homes and schools. They learn new songs and games.

Scouts work together. They play together. They make friends with people from around the world.

To Help You Remember

1. Who belongs to the Scouts?
2. What do Scouts do?

News of the World

People need to know about other countries. Sometimes they read books. Books tell about many places on Earth.

Around the world, people read newspapers. Newspapers tell what is happening in many countries.

Sometimes people need news quickly. Then they watch TV. **Satellites** help TV signals travel around the world.

A satellite is an object that is sent into space on a rocket. It is put in orbit around Earth.

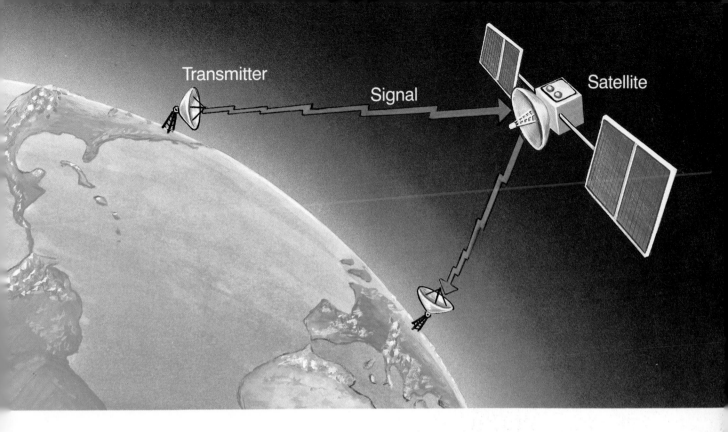

Transmitter

Signal

Satellite

A TV station sends signals to the satellite. Then the satellite sends the signals to another station. That station can be in any country on Earth.

Now people can watch what is happening anywhere on Earth.

To Help You Remember

1. Name three ways people learn about other countries.
2. How do people get the news quickly?

Unit Review

Words to Know

Choose the right words to finish each sentence.

1. A satellite ___.
2. Trading partners ___.
3. A continent ___.

a. orbits Earth
b. is a large body of land with water all around it
c. are communities that buy and sell goods from each other

Reviewing Main Ideas

A. The United States and Mexico are trading partners.
   What does Mexico sell to the United States?
   What does Mexico buy from the United States?

B. The United States and Canada work together.
   What is the Saint Lawrence Seaway?
   How does it help both countries?

C. Countries around the world trade goods.
   What else can they share?
   Why are satellites and newspapers important to people around the world?

Keeping Skills Sharp

Match the words to the colors on the map.

1. Canada   **2.** United States   **3.** Mexico

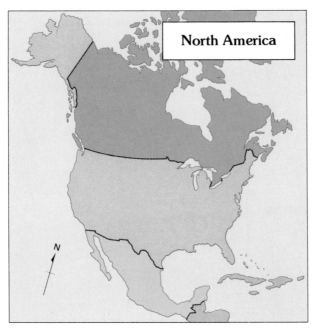

North America

Challenge!

We use things that come from far away. Read the labels on cans and boxes to find out where things are made.

1. Which come from other states? Name the states.

2. Which come from other countries? Name the countries.

Atlas

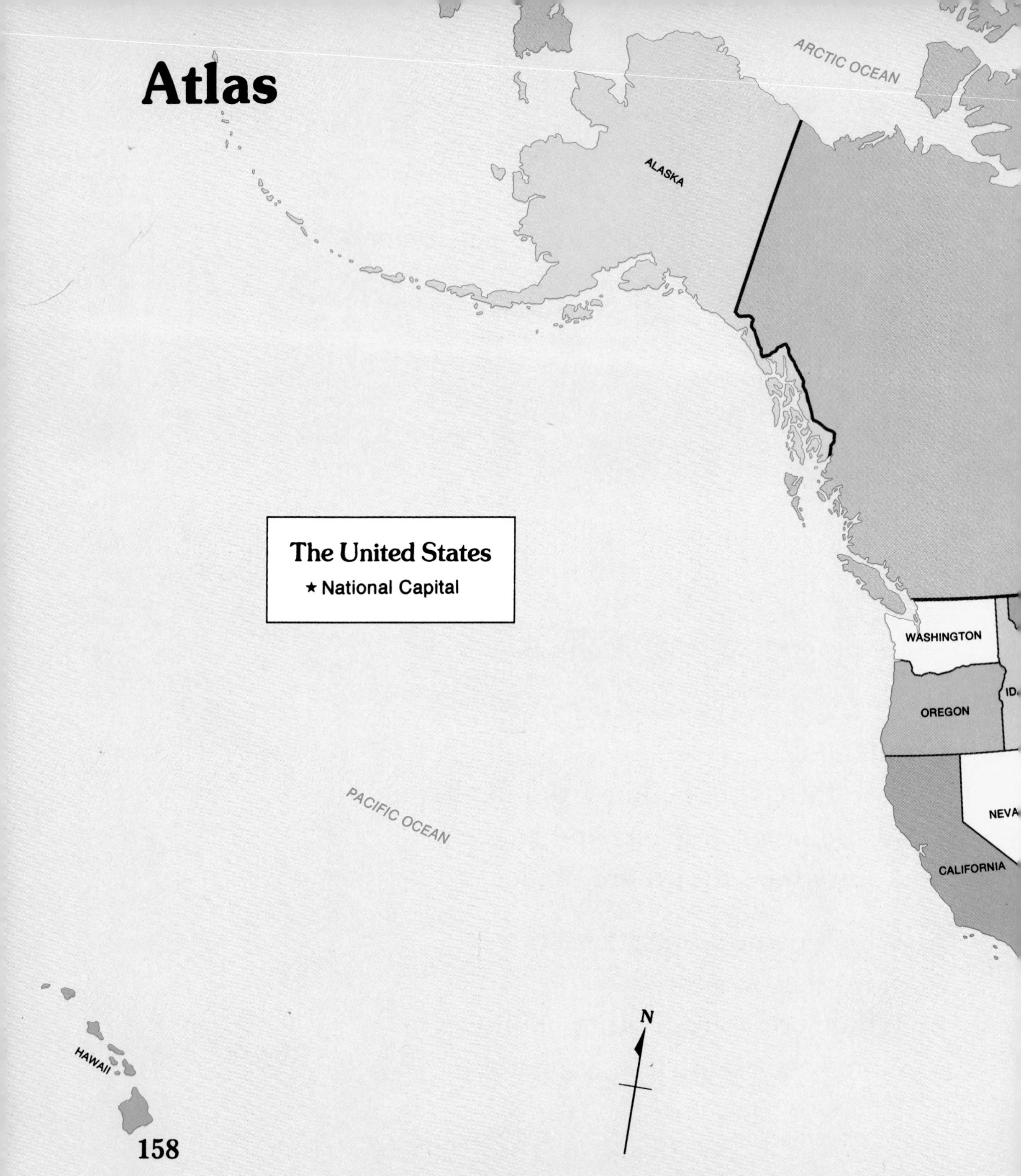

ALASKA

The United States

★ National Capital

WASHINGTON

OREGON

ID

NEVA

CALIFORNIA

PACIFIC OCEAN

N

HAWAII

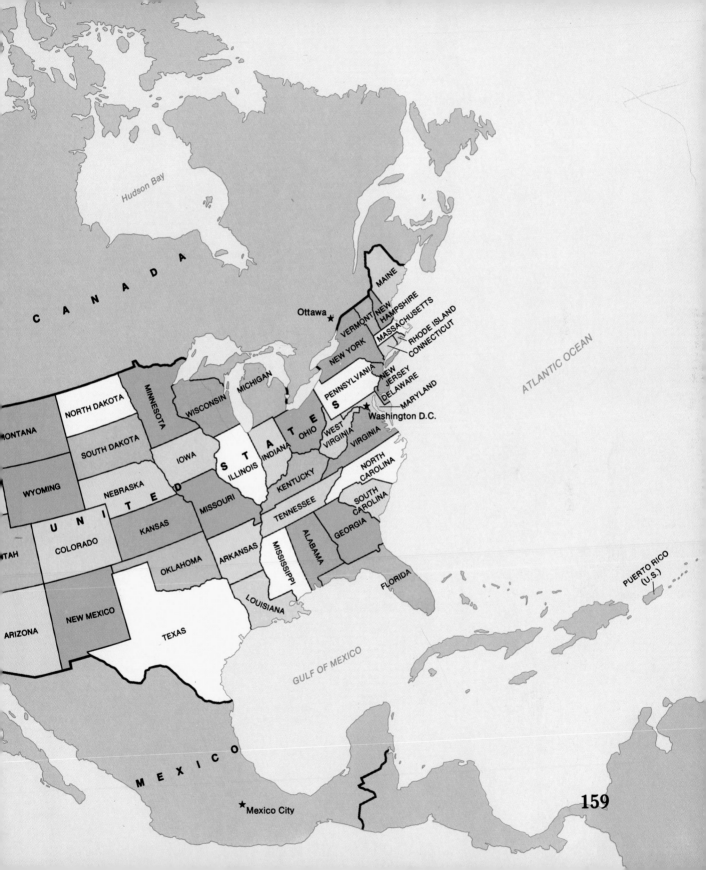

CANADA

Hudson Bay

Ottawa ★

ATLANTIC OCEAN

MONTANA

NORTH DAKOTA

MINNESOTA

WISCONSIN

MICHIGAN

MAINE

VERMONT
NEW HAMPSHIRE

MASSACHUSETTS

RHODE ISLAND
CONNECTICUT

NEW YORK

SOUTH DAKOTA

IOWA

U N I T E D

S T A T E S

PENNSYLVANIA

NEW JERSEY

DELAWARE

MARYLAND

Washington D.C. ★

WYOMING

NEBRASKA

ILLINOIS

INDIANA

OHIO

WEST VIRGINIA

VIRGINIA

UTAH

COLORADO

KANSAS

MISSOURI

KENTUCKY

TENNESSEE

NORTH CAROLINA

SOUTH CAROLINA

ARIZONA

NEW MEXICO

OKLAHOMA

ARKANSAS

MISSISSIPPI

ALABAMA

GEORGIA

TEXAS

LOUISIANA

FLORIDA

PUERTO RICO (U.S.)

GULF OF MEXICO

M E X I C O

Mexico City ★

159

The World

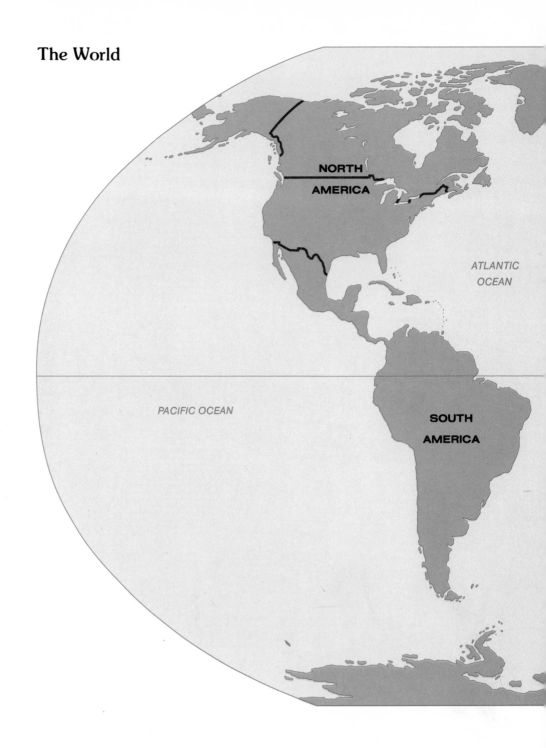

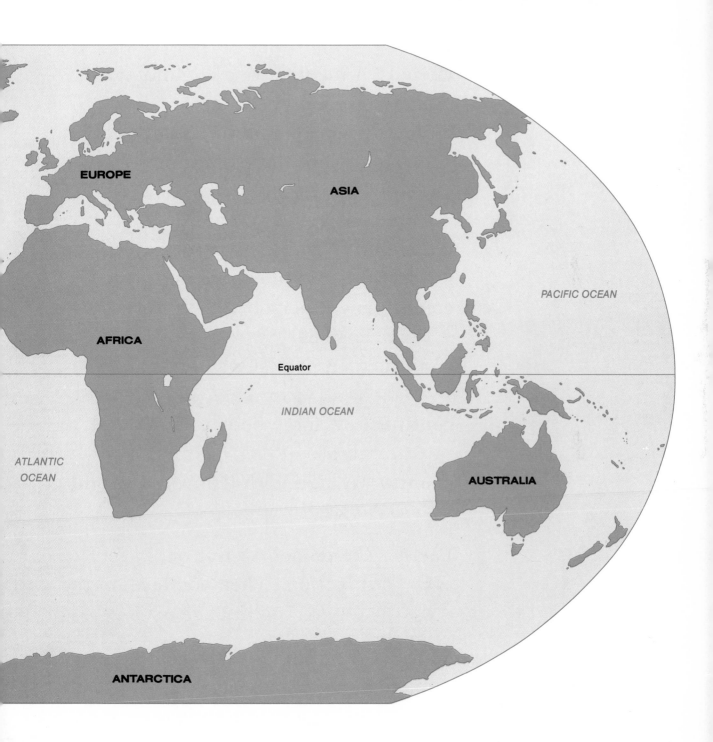

EUROPE

ASIA

AFRICA

Equator

PACIFIC OCEAN

INDIAN OCEAN

ATLANTIC
OCEAN

AUSTRALIA

ANTARCTICA

161

Words to Know

continent

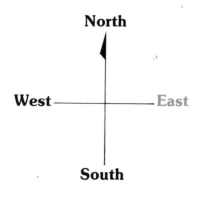

citizen   A member of a community, state, or country. Page 94

city   A large community. Many people live and work there. Page 69

climate   The weather you can count on from year to year. Page 22

community   A place where people live and work and play together. Page 35

commuter   A person who travels to work. Page 84

consumer   A person who buys and uses goods or services. Page 78

continent   A large body of land with water all around it. Page 142

country   A land with its own laws and flag. Page 101

Earth   The planet we live on. Page 9

east   A direction. When you face north, east is to your right. Page 62

factory   A building where goods are made by machine. Page 72

farm   A place where people raise many animals or grow crops. Page 54

flag A piece of cloth that stands for a country. Page 103

flag

globe A model of Earth. Page 20

goods Things people make or grow. Food and clothes are goods. Page 78

hill High land that is not as tall as a mountain. Page 13

key The part of a map that shows what symbols stand for. Page 42

lake A body of water with land all around it. Page 16

law A rule of a community, state, or country. Page 94

globe

map A drawing of a place. Page 42

mountain Very high land. Page 12

north A direction. It is toward the North Pole. Page 20

ocean A very large body of salt water. Oceans cover much of Earth. Page 15

pipeline Pipes that carry oil across the country. Page 129

plain Flat land. Page 14

map

resource

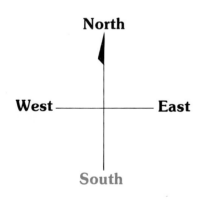
North
West —— East
South

president The person who leads the United States government. Page 112

producer A person who makes or grows something. Farmers and factory workers are producers. Page 57

ranch A large farm where animals are raised and crops are grown. Page 122

resource A part of Earth people use. Trees and oil are resources. Page 26

river A stream of water that runs from high land to low land. Page 17

satellite An object that orbits around Earth. It is sent into space on a rocket. Page 155

school A place for teaching and learning. Page 44

service worker A person who does work that helps others. Teachers, police, and people who fix cars are service workers. Page 59

south A direction. It is toward the South Pole. Page 20

state A part of our country. The United States has 50 states. Page 102

store   A place that sells goods. Page 46

suburb   A community near a large city.
Page 83

symbol   A line, dot, or picture on a
map that stands for a real thing.
Page 42

tax   Money people pay to their
community, state, or country. Page 61

town   A small community. Page 55

trade   To buy or sell. Giving money or
goods to get other goods. Page 47

trading partners   Communities that
buy and sell goods from each other.
Page 146

transportation   A way of moving things
or people from one place to another.
Page 119

travel   To go from place to place.
Page 74

vote   To make a choice. Page 95

west   A direction. When you face north,
west is to your left. Page 62

trade

North

West ———— East

South

ACKNOWLEDGEMENTS

Design Credits *Photo/Art Coordination:* Connie Komack   *Art Editing:* Penny Peters   *Photo Research:* Carole Frohlich

Cover: Betty Crowell
Unit Openers: Andrew Z. Shiff
Maps: Dick and John Sanderson, Bob Botsford and Helen McDermott (42–43, 62–63, 77, 81). James Teason (92, 93).
Graphs: Omnigraphics, Inc.

Illustration Credits 19, 32; James Teason. 36.: Tony D'Adamo (Networkgraphics). 37: Ron Toelke. 38–41, 42, 44: Tony D'Adamo (Networkgraphics). 45: Ron Toelke. 46–48, 50: Tony D'Adamo (Networkgraphics). 51: James Teason. 67, 72–73, 75, 78–79, 90–91, 99: Katy Linnett. 106–107, 130–131: Marvin Fryer (Graphics II). 155: David Hannum. 162–165: Andrew Z. Shiff.

Photo Credits Unit One: 10, 11: NASA. 12: Rick McIntyre (Tom Stack & Associates). 13, 14: Grant Heilman Photography. 15: Des & Jen Bartlett (Bruce Coleman Inc.). 16: Keith Gunnar (Bruce Coleman Inc.). 17: Grant Heilman Photography. 18: *t* DPI; *b* Bohdan Hrynewych (Southern Light). 22: *l* Eugene Luttenberg (Art Resource, Inc.); *r* Jim Smith (Art Resource, Inc.). 23: © 1978 James N. Butler. 24: Ference Berko (DPI). 25: M.P.L. Fogden (Bruce Coleman Inc.). 26: *tl, tm* Tom Magno; *tr* Steve Owlett (Bruce Coleman Inc.); *bl* John Blaustein (Woodfin Camp & Associates); *bm, br* Tom Magno. 27: *tl* Bruce A. Iverson; *tr* Jim Bradshaw; *ml* © 1982 Susan Lapides; *mr* Cliff Keeney (Lightwave); *bl* Bruce J. Nelson (Shostal Associates); *br* Christopher Cunningham. 28: *t* Robin Smith (FPG); *b* Robert Rathe (FPG). 29: © 1982 John Bradley (Positive Images). 30: John Running. 31: *l* Runk/Schoenberger (Grant Heilman Photography); *r* Daniel S. Brody (Stock, Boston). 33: *l* Brian Parker (Tom Stack & Associates; *tm* Carroll Seghers II (Leo de Wys Inc.); *tr* Clyde Smith (Peter Arnold, Inc.); *br* Peter Vandermark (Stock, Boston).

Unit Two: 45, 49: Library of Congress.

Unit Three: 54, 55: Mike Chiaverina. 56: *t* John Colwell (Grant Heilman Photography); *bl* A. M. Wattach (Shostal Associates); *br* John Messineo. 57: *l* William E. Ferguson; *r* J. C. Allen & Son. 58: Mike Chiaverina. 59: *l* Mike Chiaverina; *r* J.C. Allen and Son. 60: *l* Paul Fusco (Magnum); *r* Bohdan Hrynewych (Southern Light). 61: *tl* Rick Friedman (The Picture Cube); *tr* Roger A. Clark, Jr. (Photo Researchers, Inc.); *b* Andrew Brilliant & Carol Palmer. 64: *l* Mike Chiaverina; *r* National 4-H Council. 65: Robert Barclay (Grant Heilman Photography).

Unit Four: 70: Peter Buckley (Photo Researchers, Inc.). 71: E. R. Degginger. 74: Scott Thode (International Stock). 75: Norman Prince. 80: *t* Michael Philip Manheim (Photo Researchers, Inc.); *m* Victoria Arlak; John Coletti (Stock, Boston).

Unit Five: 84: E. Johnson (Leo de Wys Inc.). 85: *t* Michal Heron (Monkmeyer Press); *b* Andrew Brillant & Carol Palmer. 86: *t* George Hall (Woodfin Camp & Associates); *b* © 1983 Jerry Howard (Positive Images). 87: *t* E. R. Degginger; *b* Ringling Bros.-Barnum & Bailey Combined Shows, Inc. 88, 89: Andrew Brilliant & Carol Palmer. 94: *tl* Michal Heron; *tr* Syd Greenberg (DPI); *bl* Betty Crowell; *bm* Frank Cezus (Black Star); *br* Mike Mazzaschi (Stock, Boston). 95: Diana Walker (Liaison). 96: Stockphotos, Inc.

Unit Six: 102: *t* Paul Conklin; *ml* Bohdan Hrynewych (Southern Light); *mm* Michael D. Sullivan; *mr* John Messineo; *bm* Paul Conklin; *br* Donald Dietz (Stock, Boston). 103: *t* Brett (Liaison); *b* Tom Stack (Tom Stack & Associates). 107: W. S. Nawrocki. 108: Tom Magno. 110: Jerry Howard (Positive Images). 111: *l* Jerry Howard (Positive Images); *r* Tom Tracy (FPG). 112: Diego Goldberg (Sygma). 113: Michael D. Sullivan. 114: *l* E. R. Degginger; *r* detail from "George Washington" by Gilbert Stuart. Jointly owned by the Museum of Fine Arts, Boston and the National Portrait Gallery. Courtesy, Museum of Fine Arts, Boston. 115, 116: Runk/Schoenberger (Grant Heilman Photography). 117: *t* Billy E. Barnes; *b* Jerry Howard (Positive Images).

Unit Seven: 120: Larry Smith (DPI). 121: Breck P. Kent. 122: Bryce Flynn (Picture Group). 123: *l* E. R. Degginger; *r* Tom Tracy (Photophile). 124, 125: Donald L. Miller (Monkmeyer Press). 126: Richard Weiss (Peter Arnold, Inc.). 127: *t* Phil Degginger; *b* Erik Anderson. 128: Joe Rychetnik (Photo Researchers). 129: ProPix (Monkmeyer Press). 132: *t* Jerry Howard (Positive Images); *bl* Jim Foote; *br* Bill Grimes (Leo de Wys Inc.). 133, 134: Ron Garrison, Zoological Society of San Diego. 134–135: Paul Johnson. 135: *t* Andrew Brilliant & Carol Palmer; *bl* Ron Garrison, Zoological Society of San Diego; *br* M. Timothy O'Keefe (Tom Stack & Associates). 136: *t* Eric Roth, courtesy of WCVB-TV, Boston; *b* Ron Garrison, Zoological Society of San Diego. 137: *l* Tom Stack (Tom Stack & Associates); *r* Brian Parker (Tom Stack & Associates). 138: *ur* J. Gordon Miller (The Picture Cube); *tl* Tom Tracy (Photophile); *bl* D. C. Lowe (Shostal Associates); *bm* Tom Magno; *br* Neil Menschel (Picture Group).

Unit Eight: 145: *l* Andrew Brilliant & Carol Palmer; *r* E. R. Degginger. 146: *l* John Deere & Company; *r* Peter Menzel. 148: Howard Sochurek, *Life Magazine,* © Time Inc. 149: St. Lawrence Seaway Authority. 150: Girl Scouts of the U.S.A. 151: *l* Boy Scouts of America. 151*r*, 152: World Organization of the Scout Movement. 153: J. P. Defail (Photo Researchers, Inc.). 154: Alan Zlotky (Black Star).

166